GW00391843

THE
Archive Photographs
SERIES

THE CITY OF
LONDON

Ludgate Hill, *c.* 1912. The spire of the Wren church of St Martin-within-Ludgate and the dome of St Paul's Cathedral look down on a typically bustling City street scene. (© Judges Postcards, Hastings)

THE
Archive Photographs
SERIES
THE CITY OF
LONDON

Compiled by
Brian Girling

CHALFORD

First published 1998
Copyright © Brian Girling, 1998

Tempus Publishing Ltd
The Mill, Brimscombe Port,
Stroud, Gloucestershire, GL5 2QG

ISBN 0 7524 1036 9

Typesetting and origination by
Tempus Publishing Ltd
Printed in Great Britain by
Bailey Print, Dursley, Gloucestershire

Queen Victoria Street near Queen Street, c. 1920. The history of many City streets can be traced back to the thirteenth century or earlier, but Queen Victoria Street is something of a newcomer, having been laid out as part of a great Victorian road improvement during the 1860s. Its Victorian character was still apparent in this view, but that would change following war damage and rebuilding from the 1950s.

Contents

Spital Yard, Spitalfields, August 1908. Spitalfields was noted for its fruit and vegetable market which was set up in 1682 and for its Georgian terraces, many of which housed French Huguenot silk weavers and merchants who settled here around the same period. The streets ranged from the grandiose Spital Square which lost most of its houses during the present century to narrow courts and culs-de-sac like Spital Yard, shown here undergoing a facelift. A City Corporation blue plaque on a house behind the photographer marks the birthplace of Susanna Annesley, mother of John Wesley, founder of Methodism. The houses in the background in the western arm of Spital Square were later removed for street widening and an extension to Spitalfields Market. The market was acquired by the Corporation of London in 1920 but moved away in 1991. Since its foundation in 1977, the Spitalfields Historic Buildings Trust has saved numerous endangered houses in this unique corner of old London.

Introduction

London was nearly 1,800 years old when in 1839 one of the first photographs of the capital was created. We must rely on paintings and drawings to see how London looked before that, but of course, we have no contemporary pictures of Londinium, the town founded by the Romans around 43 AD and abandoned by them some 400 years later, or Lundenwic, the Saxon town built outside the Roman city wall.

With the advent of photography, London began to be pictured with an all-seeing accuracy – before this, we had to rely on what the artist chose to show us. The first photographs of the City of London, the historic, geographic and financial heart of England's greatest city and port, showed a cityscape of low-rise Georgian buildings, many dating from the rebuilding of London following the Great Fire in 1666. The skyline was punctuated by the spires and steeples of a seemingly impossible number of historic churches above which the commanding presence of St Paul's Cathedral dominated everything.

Photography arrived in time to record the virtual rebuilding of the City by the Victorians as the dignified Georgian buildings gave way to the stolid stone-fronted constructions that reflected the City's nineteenth-century prosperity. The rise of the capital's vast public transport system was similarly recorded, as were the great road-building schemes which cut through mazes of medieval streets at the heart of the City.

By the end of the nineteenth century, with photography an increasingly affordable process, an innovation spread to this country from the continent which would bring photography to the attention of everyone – the picture postcard. In 1894, a reluctant Post Office finally agreed that the previously plain postcards could now carry pictures as had been allowed abroad. The new pictorial cards caught everyone's imagination and as the Edwardian era dawned, Britain was turned into a nation of collectors as just about everything that was of any interest to anybody was pictured on a postcard. Combining the pretty with the practical, cards could be sent anywhere in the world for a penny and anywhere in this country for a halfpenny. In those distant days, there was, of course, no television and few newspapers carried pictures, and for a while the humble postcard fulfilled a role that would later be taken by photo-journalism. Postcard photographs of local events were produced and on sale within hours and the super-efficient Edwardian postal system allowed them to be bought, written, posted and delivered on the same day. Most families had a postcard album, which was often a picture gallery of Edwardian life, its content dependent upon the tastes and circumstances of its owners.

With its unique historic attractions, ceremonies and events, the City of London was pictured by a multitude of postcard photographers and publishers (over seventy of whom were based in the City), and it is from this legacy that much of the collection in this book has been compiled. National and international publishers included the City as part of their series of cards, and although many were mass-produced and uninspiring, others brought a more individual style that lifted them above the run of the mill. Notable among the publishers were the Parisian firm of Lucien Levy who produced beautifully printed postcards of London (p. 20), and Raphael Tuck & Sons Ltd who from 1900 onwards produced a vast quantity of high quality London views (p. 79). Other publishers included John Beagles & Co. Ltd and the Rotary Photographic Co. Ltd, whose output included fine series of London's street characters and royal events (pp. 44, 45, 77), and historic London (pp. 124, 125). The Photochrom Co. Ltd also had a prolific output over several decades, and in the 1940s produced series of City war ruins that had to be approved by the Censor (p. 19).

The photographers themselves were adept at tailoring their own styles for the postcard, notably Fredrick Judge who founded the firm of Judges of Hastings which is still producing high quality postcards. The Judges cards were finished in their distinctive rich sepia and were characterized by their adventurous compositions, unusual viewpoints and carefully chosen lighting conditions (e.g. pp. 30, 40).

During the 1920s, the partnership of Messrs Degen and Lewis of Nottingham produced some of the best postcards of that decade, with a wonderful run of superbly detailed views that captured the atmosphere of the working City, with teeming streets filled with animation and, to us, antiquated traffic (e.g. pp. 9, 55, 98). There was also room in the City for local photographers like Arthur Witts of the Temple, whose activities were confined to that venerable lawyer's precinct (pp. 16, 17), and Joseph Neal of St Dunstan's Hill. His patch included the lively Billingsgate fish market and the narrow lanes in the south east of the City. Many cards carried no identification as to their origin, while others exploited a rich vein of Edwardian nostalgia for corners of old London that had vanished in Victorian times (p. 52).

City postcards also chart the arrival of the railways, the replacement of malodorous steam-driven Underground trains by new electric ones, and new motor buses to oust the antiquated Victorian horse buses. In the City's financial heart, the business of the day was conducted from solid low-rise buildings, which contrast with today's glittering towers of high finance. Londoners crowded the City's markets; Farringdon has closed, ancient Billingsgate moved away, but Smithfield endures as does the Cockneys' favourite, Petticoat Lane.

Since then, much of the City has changed out all recognition following the devastation of the Blitz and the rebuilding afterwards, but a walk through the ancient 'Square Mile' will still reveal many hidden corners of the old City, aided by the City Corporation's informative 'blue plaques' which are to be found everywhere. Our postcards show us wonderful places that have been lost, but also the rediscovery of treasures from London's past, like the Mithraic temple from Roman Londinium, and parts of the Roman wall emerging from centuries of accumulated debris, unseen, perhaps, for a thousand years. Most of the photographs are appearing in print here for the first time, and reproductions of many of them are available from Brian Girling, 17 Devonshire Road, Harrow HA1 4LS.

Fleet Street and Ludgate Circus, *c.* 1910. Note that there was still room for a cab rank in the middle of Edwardian Fleet Street.

One
Around Fleet Street

Ludgate Circus from Fleet Street, *c*. 1919. Fleet Street, the ancient route between the cities of London and Westminster, runs from Temple Bar to Ludgate Circus, where it slopes down into the valley of the river from which it takes its name. The street was called Fleetbridge Street from the wooden bridge which crossed the river close to the location of this photograph, but the river now flows underground beneath Farringdon Street and New Bridge Street. Fleet Street is famed worldwide for its association with printing and newspapers which dates back to around 1500 when Wynkyn de Worde, a protégé of pioneer printer William Caxton, set up his press in Shoe Lane. London's first daily newspaper, the *Daily Courant,* was published from 1702 in a house by what is now Ludgate Circus. In more recent times, decentralization has stripped the 'Street of Ink' of its scribes and printers, leaving only romantic memories and the odd name of a long-departed publication still visible on an old frontage. At its western end, Fleet Street means 'Legal London', with the stunning Victorian Gothic Royal Courts of Justice at the City boundary. To the south, the ancient legal precinct of the Temple with its barristers' chambers runs down to the Embankment, while to the north the legal enclaves of Lincoln's Inn and Gray's Inn make a remarkable and beautiful townscape.

Old Temple Bar from Fleet Street, *c.* 1876. Temple Bar is the western boundary of the City of London, and up to the fourteenth century was marked by nothing more than a chain across the road. From then onwards, the road was guarded by a gate topped by a prison, and in 1670, the elegant structure we see here was built. Increasing volumes of traffic were seriously impeded by the narrow archway, and Temple Bar was dismantled to be re-erected at Theobald's Park, Hertfordshire. Plans to return it to the City have yet to come to fruition. Old property to the right of the view would soon be replaced by the new Royal Courts of Justice.

'The Griffin', Temple Bar, Fleet Street, *c.* 1920. A similar viewpoint reveals a widened Fleet Street, and the Royal Courts of Justice which were completed in 1882. The site of Temple Bar is marked by a memorial of 1880 topped by the City's winged dragon emblem, popularly called 'The Griffin'. Middle Temple Gateway, which dates from 1684, is at the far left of both views.

The Royal Courts of Justice (the Law Courts), c. 1902. The Law Courts were designed by G.E. Street and were built between 1874 and 1882 on the site of a notorious slum. The spectacular Gothic buildings replaced the old Law Courts next to Westminster Hall, which were promptly demolished. Every year, during the Lord Mayor's show, the new Lord Mayor of London swears an oath of allegiance to the sovereign at the Law Courts.

Prince Henry's Room, Fleet Street, c. 1920. This old house was built in 1611 and once formed part of a row of similarly gabled and timbered buildings. The house was used by Prince Henry, the Prince of Wales, son of James I. Under less exalted ownership it later became a pub, a waxworks, and a hairdressing salon. The house was reconstructed in 1906, but still contains some original Jacobean panelling and a Jacobean plaster ceiling. It now houses an exhibition of memorabilia associated with diarist Samuel Pepys. The stone archway dated 1748 is an entrance to the Temple, and in 1905 the building on the left housed the first office of the Automobile Association.

Inner Temple Hall, *c.* 1910. The name derives from the Knights Templar of St John of Jerusalem, a religious order set up to protect pilgrims on their way to the Holy Land. In the twelfth century they acquired land between the Thames and Fleet Street but the order was suppressed and the land was transferred to the Knights Hospitallers who took lawyers as their tenants, thereby beginning the tradition of legal occupation of the Temple. Today, the Temple remains an oasis of peace and tranquillity and, although ravaged by the Blitz, the spectacular halls can still be seen. Inner Temple Hall was built between 1868 and 1870 and rebuilt in 1955 following wartime destruction. The hall faced the lawns where the Royal Horticultural Society held their annual show until it moved westwards in 1913 to become the Chelsea Flower Show.

Lamb Building and Inner Temple Hall, *c.* 1908. Lamb Building dates from 1667 and stood between Temple Church and Inner Temple Hall. A tablet among the paving stones of Church Court now marks the site of the block of lawyers' chambers which was not rebuilt following its wartime destruction.

Pump Court from the Cloisters, c. 1908. With its venerable buildings, secluded courts and narrow lanes, the Temple conveys something of the atmosphere of a historic university town. Pump Court typifies the tranquil nature of the place, and although partly rebuilt from 1951 to 1953 following war damage, it remains little different from this atmospheric scene from ninety years ago. In common with the rest of the Temple, it is still illuminated by its Victorian gas lamps. (© Judges Postcards, Hastings)

Making wigs in the Temple, *c.* 1920. This multi-talented gentleman was Arthur R. Witts, who in addition to his skills as a wig maker, had similar expertise in photography. His photographs of the Temple were printed as postcards and were sold from his shop in Middle Temple Lane where solicitors' robes were also available. Mr Witts took this photograph himself.

Arthur Witt's shop, Middle Temple Lane, *c.* 1926. The crowded shop window, stacked high with photographs, postcards and wigs, overlooked the Fleet Street end of Middle Temple Lane which was so narrow that there was no room for a pavement. Visitors to the Temple could purchase guide books and other souvenirs from the shop, which was a fascinating place in its own right, and a good starting point from which to explore the delights of the Temple.

Cloisters, The Temple, *c.* 1920. Part of Temple Church is seen beyond the seventeenth-century Cloisters, which contained another wig shop, that of Messrs Savage & Smith, centre left. The shady Cloisters, where the legal fraternity would once stroll after the day's work, were destroyed during the Second World War and rebuilt afterwards. The foundation stone was laid on 20 March 1951.

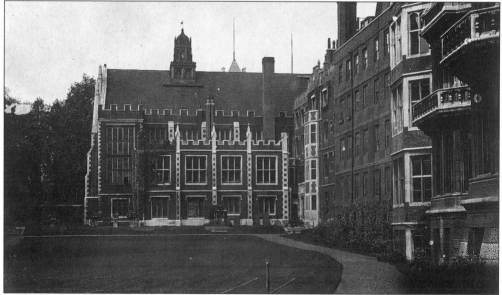

Middle Temple Hall from Middle Temple Gardens, *c.* 1920. The hall was built during the reign of Elizabeth I and still contains the massive table made of oak from Windsor Great Park, a gift from Her Majesty. Early in the seventeenth century, Queen Elizabeth attended the first presentation of Shakespeare's *Twelfth Night* at Middle Temple Hall. Although it suffered war damage, the hall has been restored, and is one of the treasures of the Temple.

Middle Temple Lane and Hare Court from Brick Court, *c.* 1920. Although Middle Temple Lane opens out by Brick Court, its upper end retains the appearance of a City street from before the Great Fire of London in 1666. The houses here overhang the lane and were built of wood and plaster in contravention of a post-Fire regulation which dictated that all new buildings should be of brick or stone. This picturesque group has, however, survived having outlasted the majority of those built in the 'correct' manner. Dr Samuel Johnson, lexicographer and compiler of the famous dictionary, had rooms at No. 2 Middle Temple Lane. Hare Court, right, is a Victorian rebuilding of a part of the Temple where Judge Jeffreys, whose harsh judgements at the Bloody Assize earned him considerable notoriety, had rooms.

War ruins from Middle Temple Lane, *c.* 1948. The Second World War left the Temple in a sorry state, with both Inner Temple Hall and Temple Church burnt and roofless. Part of Pump Court and the Cloisters has gone but the Victorian Farrar's Building, left, has survived. By the end of the 1940s, a rebuilding programme had begun to return the Temple to something like its former state, and to close off the new, shocking, vistas where familiar landmarks had once been. The foreground of this view would soon be occupied by the neo-Georgian Harcourt Buildings.

Temple Church, *c.* 1945. The round church was built by the Knights Templar in the twelfth century, its shape being inspired by that of the Church of the Holy Sepulchre in Jerusalem. The church still contains stonework from the twelfth century, together with the alterations and additions of the following centuries, and the famous effigies of twelfth-century knights. The air raids of 1941 left the church in the state we see it here, but restoration has returned Temple Church to its former splendour.

18

Clifford's Inn, *c.* 1910. This former Inn of Chancery lay to the north of Fleet Street by Fetter Lane. It was named after Robert de Clifford whose widow leased it to law students from 1345. Clifford's Inn stood until 1934 when its mainly eighteenth-century buildings were demolished. Flats and offices were built on the site. Writers Virginia and Leonard Woolf, founders of the Hogarth Press, lived in Clifford's Inn in 1912-13.

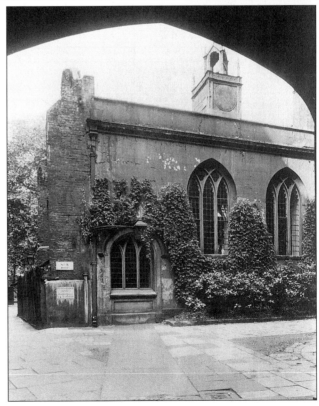

The Old Hall, Clifford's Inn, *c.* 1918. This was the oldest part of Clifford's Inn, where in 1670 judges met to settle boundary disputes arising from the Great Fire of London. Having raged through the City for five days, the Great Fire burnt itself out near Clifford's Inn and Fleet Street. Two ancient houses that survived the Fire still stand near Temple Bar.

Fleet Street, *c.* 1918. Many of these varied frontages on the north side of Fleet Street can still be seen, but the newspapers and magazines that were based here have all gone. The photograph antedates the rebuilding in more grandiose style of the premises of two national dailies, *The Daily Telegraph*, with its large clock, and the *Daily Express* whose new building in the 1930s featured an eye-catching display of black glass. This part of Fleet Street is notable for the ancient passages and alleys running beneath the buildings. Wine Office Court, where the historic Ye Olde Cheshire Cheese pub stands, is at the centre of the view.

Another panorama of press offices and the typically lively street life of Fleet Street, looking west in around 1912. The block of buildings on the right was replaced in 1931 by the new *Daily Express* headquarters.

Ye Olde Cheshire Cheese, Wine Office Court, *c.* 1910. Around Fleet Street the written word ruled and a number of famous literary figures have lived here including Dr Samuel Johnson, who had addresses in Middle Temple Lane and Gough Square. His 'local' was Ye Olde Cheshire Cheese, a venerable hostelry which also had connections with Thackeray, Goldsmith and Dickens.

The bar of Ye Olde Cheshire Cheese, *c.* 1910. The old-world ambience of this much loved pub, which was rebuilt within a year of its destruction in the Great Fire, makes it a firm favourite with visitors and locals alike.

The *Daily Express* building, c. 1934. With its shiny black glass, chromium strips and streamlined appearance, the *Daily Express* building of 1931 brought a dramatic foretaste of modern architecture to the sober façades of Fleet Street. *The Daily Telegraph* also rebuilt on a grand scale, but in a more traditional style, in 1928, but both buildings were abandoned as the newspapers left Fleet Street.

Looking towards Fleet Street from the church of St Andrew-by-the-Wardrobe, c. 1931. The City of the 1930s was mostly Victorian in appearance, with a scattering of survivals from previous centuries. All that changed with the air raids of the Second World War and post-war building schemes which gave the City a new face of high-tech office blocks. The last decade of the old City is pictured here, with a seemingly chaotic jumble of historic streets and lanes above which the wedding-cake spire of St Bride's, Fleet Street, rises clear and unobstructed. St Bride's was rebuilt by Wren after the Fire, with a celebrated spire, which at 226 ft high is the tallest of Wren's church spires. The site of St Bride's is of the greatest historical interest, with evidence of Roman, Saxon, Norman and medieval constructions beneath the church. To the right, the large lettering highlights the premises of Gerrish, Ames & Simpkins Ltd, wholesale clothiers of Carter Lane, a part of the City where the narrow streets still have many of their older buildings. Fleet Street is seen in the distant centre of the view, with the tall, white *Daily Telegraph* building standing high above its neighbours. A constructor's crane rises above the *Daily Express* building, then nearing completion. Further back is the square tower of the Public Record Office in Chancery Lane, and the needle spire of the Law Courts on the horizon to the left.

Ludgate Circus and Ludgate Hill from Fleet Street, c. 1908. The circus still has a Victorian look about it today, but the south eastern quadrant seen here with its electric Bovril and Schweppes advertisements has been removed, as has the adjoining railway bridge.

Ludgate Circus and Fleet Street from Ludgate Hill, c. 1908. This unusual view of Ludgate Circus was taken from underneath the railway bridge built in 1866 to carry the London, Chatham and Dover railway northwards to Farringdon Street, where it linked with the then new Metropolitan railway. At ground level there is the usual Edwardian free-for-all, with pedestrians dodging the traffic, and a policeman keeping an eye on things from beside the memorial obelisk to former Lord Mayor Robert Waithman to the right. Ludgate Circus was not famous for its bright lights, but in 1908 the electric signs rivalled those of Piccadilly Circus.

24

Two
The River Thames

London Bridge, c. 1905. The first bridge crossing of the great river the Romans called Tamesis was made at the furthest point downstream where firm ground amid the surrounding marshland allowed the construction of a pair of bridgeheads. With higher ground close by, two hills beside a stream (later called Walbrook), it was a good place for the new settlement. Londinium, the Roman town, was well placed for maritime trade with the rest of Europe via the river and for road communications with the rest of the Roman province of Britannia and its prosperity was assured. The early bridges were short-lived wooden affairs, but in 1176 a new London Bridge was begun, which would last until 1831 when its replacement, built a few yards upstream by Sir John Rennie, opened. This is the bridge we see here, which served the City well until a plain concrete structure replaced it in 1972. The fine old Rennie bridge was dismantled and rebuilt at Lake Havasu, Arizona. The picture captures the daily invasion of commuters as they head towards their toil in the City from London Bridge Station. To the left is the hall of the Worshipful Company of Fishmongers, one of the city's ancient Livery Companies. The dagger with which the Lord Mayor of London stabbed Wat Tyler, leader of the Peasants' Revolt in 1381, is on view here.

Tower Bridge, *c.* 1910. Until 1991 when the Queen Elizabeth II Bridge opened at Dartford, Tower Bridge was the first Thames bridge on the seaward side of London. It was opened in 1894 by the Prince of Wales, later Edward VII. The eye-catching new bridge replaced the Tower Subway, a tunnel between Bermondsey and Tower Hill which had opened in 1869. Victorian Londoners were transported beneath the Thames in a cable-hauled tramcar, but this was withdrawn after three months and one had then to walk through.

Tower Bridge, *c.* 1910. From the river, Tower Bridge makes the most impressive of gateways to the Upper Pool, where cargoes from all over the world were once handled by the City's wharves and warehouses. The road traffic is carried on twin bascules which are raised to let taller ships through. (© Judges Postcards, Hastings)

Tower Bridge, *c.* 1920. Tower Bridge was built to relieve the pressure of road traffic on neighbouring London Bridge, and although designed during the age of horse-drawn vehicles, its massive construction has allowed it to cope well with the demands of modern road users. On the northern side, the approach road was built on part of Little Tower Hill which separated St Katharine's Docks from the Tower of London.

Sunset at Tower Bridge, *c.* 1912. The bridge's great Gothic towers rise high above the river's evening mists – a romantic image of the Thames at dusk beloved of artists and photographers who constantly strive to capture the river's moods. (© Judges Postcards, Hastings)

Tower Bridge, August 1915. A somewhat lurid picture, published in Germany during the First World War, illustrating the latest means of aerial warfare, the Zeppelin. Although parts of eastern England were damaged by these early air raids, destruction was on a modest scale when compared with the Blitz of the Second World War. London's ancient fortress, the Tower of London, is seen through the opened bascules of Tower Bridge.

The Tower of London from Tower Bridge, c. 1907. The Tower was built from around 1077 to guard the river approaches to London, and was much extended during the following centuries. The history of Britain has been bound up with the Tower, which has held the role of fortress, prison and observatory, and was a notorious place of execution. This view shows the oldest part of the Tower (other than some Roman remains), the White Tower, so named from the whitewash which once covered its walls. The walls were rather less white in the smoky air of Edwardian London.

The British and Foreign Wharf, Lower East Smithfield (St Katharine's Way), *c.* 1905. Commercial river traffic dates from London's earliest days, when Roman galleys trading with the east coast ports and the continent unloaded their cargoes at the quays and hithes of what would later become the Pool of London. By the Victorian era, the docks were at the height of their prosperity and stretched far downstream towards the Thames estuary. The 1960s saw inner London's docks in decline as heavy container traffic became more comveniently located along the river's lower reaches. This view typifies the bustling scenes of the Edwardian era, just downstream of Tower Bridge. The British and Foreign Wharf handled cargoes of wine and spirits.

Floating Customs Station, off Custom House, *c.* 1910. Customs duty on goods brought by incoming ships has been collected at Custom House since 1275, but the building itself has been rebuilt many times. The present neo-classical structure, partly seen on the left, was built in 1825. HMS *Harpy*, a floating customs station and pier, was moored along side.

Dutch eel boats off Billingsgate, *c*. 1912. Eels were once a favourite part of the Londoner's diet, and the Dutchmen found a ready market in the City for their fish. Their boats were moored off Billingsgate and the eels were sold direct from them. The view gives a good impression of how busy the river was early in the century, with Dutch eel schuyts, lighters and a sail-driven barge against a backdrop of Tower Bridge and wharves on the Bermondsey riverside. (© Judges Postcards, Hastings)

The Pool of London, *c*. 1912. Another lively scene in the Pool, with sailing barges and lighters, which were used to transfer cargoes from ship to wharf or from ship to ship. (© Judges Postcards, Hastings)

London Bridge Wharf from London Bridge, *c.* 1904. London's busy river was also used by passenger and pleasure steamers which could be boarded at London Bridge Wharf and Old Swan Pier on either side of London Bridge. The paddle steamers were highly popular as these crowded scenes confirm. Here was the site of old London Bridge, which was just east of the modern crossing.

View from London Bridge, *c.* 1908. The *London Belle* is seen with a good crowd on board all ready for a bracing cruise on the Thames. The paddle steamers called at riverside towns like Gravesend and they also served the east coast ports and the seaside towns of East Anglia and Kent. River cruises are still very popular, but the ships now use Tower Pier, which is almost directly above the line of the Victorian Tower Subway.

The City river front, *c.* 1920. Notable landmarks visible here include Custom House, right, with Billingsgate fish market to the left of it. The Monument rises high behind Custom House, while the tower of St Magnus the Martyr competes for the skyline with St Paul's Cathedral, centre. The long straight roof of Cannon Street station is seen beyond Rennie's London Bridge.

Under London Bridge, *c.* 1912. An unusual view of the Pool of London; a typical example of the work of photographer Fred Judge whose early twentieth-century views of London are renowned for their original compositions and beautiful atmospheric effects. (© Judges Postcards, Hastings)

An afternoon view on London Bridge around 1926 with home-going commuters (every one wearing a hat) making their way back to London Bridge station. To the right is Adelaide House, which had only just been completed. It was the first of the riverside office blocks in the City, and one which still stands. The building features Egyptian-style details and was something of a trend setter in its day.

A stone shelter from Old London Bridge in Victoria Park, c. 1910. Medieval London Bridge was one of the wonders of the City with picturesque timber-framed houses between which a narrow roadway carried the traffic. The old houses were removed between 1758 and 1762 and the bridge itself was demolished once Rennie's new granite structure was opened in 1831. A few remnants of the old bridge survived, including this stone alcove, which found a new role as a public shelter in Victoria Park, Hackney.

32907. London St Paul's Cath!. S.E. C.N.

Cannon Street Railway Bridge, Southwark Bridge, and St Paul's Cathedral, *c.* 1905. London Bridge was the only Thames bridge in London until Westminster's crossing opened in the 1740s. A new bridge designed by Rennie connected the City with Southwark in 1819, but this was replaced with a new Southwark Bridge in 1921. Cannon Street Railway Bridge, in the foreground, opened in 1866 and carried the South Eastern Railway into the new Cannon Street station. St Paul's Cathedral was still the dominant feature of the Edwardian City.

The City waterfront from Bankside, Southwark, *c.* 1912. The docks and wharves which crowded the riverside once made it difficult for the pedestrian to get a glimpse of the Thames except from the bridges. On the Southwark side, however, Bankside ran beside the river and gave fine views of the City from between the wharves. Bankside was once notorious for its brothels and bear baiting, but is now famed for its rebuilt Globe Theatre where Shakespeare's plays are performed much as they were during the playwright's lifetime.

The City from Bankside, *c.* 1919. Another view of the City's commercial riverside, with its narrow, shadowy lanes running between the wharves. The lanes had old-world names that recalled a rich vein of City history: Stew Lane, Broken Wharf, Trig Lane and Queenhithe, among others. There is a new riverside walkway to Blackfriars here now with attractive modern buildings including that of the City of London Boys' School, whose site was once occupied by Baynard's Castle.

St Paul's rises high above the lowlier rooftops, its dome framed by the sails of an old Thames barge, around 1915. The cathedral's architect, Sir Christopher Wren, took a house on Bankside from which he was able to view the builders' progress on his masterpiece.

A Thames river pageant near Billingsgate and Custom House, 1919. The Thames has played its part on ceremonial occasions and the Lord Mayor's Show has occasionally taken place upon its waters. In 1452, a ceremonial barge equipped with silver oars conveyed the Lord Mayor to Westminster to swear his oath of allegiance to the sovereign. In 1919, a naval pageant formed part of the peace celebrations at the end of the First World War.

Blackfriars Bridge from Blackfriars Road, c. 1907. The first Blackfriars Bridge was opened on 19 November 1769, and its successor on 6 November 1869. The bridge was widened in 1907-09 to make room for the London County Council's electric trams to cross and link up with the existing tram lines along Victoria Embankment (see p. 85). This work can be seen in progress to the left.

Blackfriars Bridge, *c.* 1909. The newly widened bridge could now accommodate the trams, the first of which crossed the Thames on 14 September 1909, the day the bridge was re-opened by the Lord Mayor of London. The Lord Mayor himself drove the first tram over the bridge. The curving façade in the background is that of the 350-bedroomed De Keyser's Royal Hotel which was built on the site of Henry VIII's Bridewell Palace, which stood by the mouth of the River Fleet. The hotel was replaced by Unilever House in 1930.

Victoria Embankment, Blackfriars, *c.* 1920. To the right of the busy tram station is the City of London School for Boys, whose building still stands following the departure of the school to new premises in Paul's Walk, the modern Thames-side path. The Blackfriars area was named after an order of Dominican or Black Friars who established a monastery nearby in the thirteenth century.

Victoria Embankment under construction, seen from Somerset House, *c.* 1864. Before the 1860s, the river front at Blackfriars looked much as it did further east with commercial and maritime activities dominating the scene. That all changed when a massive scheme of land reclamation preceded the construction of a grand riverside boulevard along the great curve of the river's north bank from Blackfriars to Westminster Bridge. It was designed by the Metropolitan Board of Works' Chief Engineer, Sir Joseph Bazalgette, and opened up a vast area of London's riverside previously hidden from view. The scheme also included a new sewerage

system and a new Underground railway. The view captures an early stage in the reclamation works, and gives a good impression of their scale. The river's waters once lapped the walls of the buildings on the left. Vanished landmarks include the Gothic Middle Temple Library (built 1858), and the City of London Gasworks, whose vapours did not improve the air quality in this part of the City. Old Blackfriars Bridge was at the end of its life, and St Paul's Cathedral, as ever in old photographs, dominates the scene. A new Underground station, Temple (then called The Temple), would open on 30 May 1870 near the centre of this view.

Sunset over Blackfriars Bridge, *c.* 1912. The transient beauty of a smoky London sunset, with dusk softening the outlines of the trio of Blackfriars Bridges (one road bridge and two railway). The silhouettes of the City of London School and De Keyser's Royal Hotel are visible beyond the sailing barges moored by the Southwark shore. (© Judges Postcards, Hastings)

'Outcasts, London, 1 a.m.', Blackfriars, *c.* 1912. The City's day is done, the last tram has gone and the rails glisten in the street lights. As a dank river fog rolls in from the Thames, a pair of benighted figures try to snatch what sleep they can on an unforgiving Embankment seat. This side of London life contrasts dramatically with the wealth and opulence of the City. (© Judges Postcards, Hastings)

40

Three
City Life

Hansom cab and District Messenger boy, Salisbury Square, *c.* 1905. The two-seater hansom cabs, with their large wheels and driver seated behind his passengers, were a familiar part of the City scene during much of the nineteenth and early twentieth centuries. The design of these 'safety cabriolets' was patented in 1834 by multi-talented Joseph Hansom, the architect who also designed Birmingham Town Hall. This picture shows another familiar character from bygone London, a District Messenger with his smart uniform. These lads performed a variety of useful tasks around London's streets including running errands and queuing for theatre tickets. The location here is Salisbury Square, close to Salisbury Court where the City's celebrated diarist Samuel Pepys was born in 1632. Pepys' eye-witness accounts of London life in the seventeenth century including the Great Plague of 1665 and Fire of 1666 have enthralled readers since their publication in 1825. Salisbury Square is now the home of the stone obelisk which commemorated the mayoralty of Robert Waithman in 1823-4 (see p. 24).

A flower-girl at the Royal Exchange, c. 1920. The Classical façade of the Royal Exchange overlooks the forecourt, where boot-blacks, newspaper sellers and cockney flower-girls plied their trades. A boot-black and client can be seen to the left of the City of London War Memorial in the centre.

A boot-black at the Royal Exchange, c. 1906. There was plenty of work for the boot-black in Edwardian London, where horse droppings and muddy roads were hazards for the unwary. This top-hatted City gent would certainly go to business clean shod. A street orderly with a broom, in the centre, was part of the vast army of people employed to keep the streets and pavements clean.

A flower-girl and client, Cheapside, *c.* 1904. A full-skirted Edwardian lady searches in her purse for some change to complete her transaction with another of the City's traditional flower-girls. The picture is called 'Roses in Cheapside' and is by City photographers A. & G. Taylor of Queen Victoria Street, who preserved many informal scenes like this.

Telegraph messenger, *c.* 1905. Uniformed youths abounded in the City: there was plenty of delivery work for boys employed by press agencies and cable companies. The telegraph messengers were frequently seen running about the City on their red Post Office bicycles.

Newspaper boys, *c*. 1908. These lads did not need a uniform, but a cloth cap and muffler were *de rigueur*. The picture recalls a time when London had three evening newspapers: the *Evening News*, the *Star* and the *Evening Standard*. It would seem from the newspaper placards that there might shortly be work for the then new Central Criminal Courts, the Old Bailey.

City Police on point duty in Queen Victoria Street in 1906, controlling the busy traffic in the days before traffic lights took over the job. Queen Victoria Street was named after the sovereign during whose reign it was built, as a continuation of the Victoria Embankment project.

City Police ambulance, *c.* 1907. City of London Police duties included the supervision of the ambulance service. This smart new battery-powered vehicle was photographed near St Bartholomew's Hospital.

Throgmorton Street from Old Broad Street, *c*. 1920. City crowds take advantage of traffic-free conditions to stroll in the roadway between typical Victorian buildings in the City's financial heart. Today, the street is still narrow, but in dramatic contrast there is a towering 320 ft high Stock Exchange in place of its predecessor on the left. The hall of the Drapers' Company, one of the City's ancient Livery Companies, is on the right, its entrance guarded, as it is today, by a pair of bearded caryatids.

Street vendors on Ludgate Hill, *c.* 1905. Amid the City's high finance, there was still room for much humbler traders to exist. Ludgate Hill was a favourite pitch for a variety of street vendors, including flower-girls, newspaper boys and trinket sellers. Here, a young man, more ambitiously set up than his fellows, appears to be having trouble finding a place for his barrow. Parking in the City could be hard to find, even in Edwardian times!

Central Meat Markets, Smithfield, *c.* 1910. London's principal wholesale meat market was opened in 1868 on the site of a horse, cattle and meat market which dated back to Norman times. 'Smithfield' is a corruption of 'Smoothfield', the location outside the City wall for what were notoriously unsanitary proceedings which lasted until 1855 when the cattle market moved to Islington. Here, a group of butchers and market porters (known as Bummarees) take a break from their labours in the cathedral-like market halls.

Farringdon Market, Smithfield, *c.* 1910. Farringdon Market was set up in Smithfield's Central Markets in 1874 having moved from former premises near Shoe Lane. These had replaced the earlier Fleet Market, and the even earlier Stocks Market, a fish and meat market established in the thirteenth century on the site of Mansion House. Farringdon Market traded in fruit, vegetables and fish and there were shops running along Farringdon Road from Charterhouse Street. That nearest the camera was Ernest Bottom's bookshop, which sold prints, maps and magazines. The shop itself has almost vanished under a mass of hanging paper.

The fish market, Farringdon Market, *c.* 1905. Oysters were sixpence a dozen at the stall of Woolven & Co., in the centre. A post-war office block, Caxton House, stands here now.

'Birch's', Cornhill, c. 1912. This exquisite little Adam shop front could once have been found at 15 Cornhill, where it contained the premises of Birch & Co., the caterers. The company was founded during the reign of Charles II, and provided splendid fare for City banquets for over 250 years. The eighteenth-century shop front is seen after restoration when, apparently, paint around $\frac{3}{4}$ inch deep was removed from the carved woodwork. The shop front was eventually acquired by the Museum of London.

Thomas Wallis', Holborn, c. 1903. Two of the City's largest stores once faced each other across Holborn: Gamage's on the north side and Thomas Wallis', the general drapers, in this vast Victorian edifice opposite. Both stores have now departed; Thomas Wallis' made a spectacular exit during an air raid on the night of 16-17 April 1941 when the building was burnt out. The site was taken by Mirror Newspapers for their headquarters from 1960. To the right by Fetter Lane was a branch of the popular bakers, the Aerated Bread Company, the once familiar 'ABC'.

Hall's shop, 84 Long Lane, Smithfield, *c*. 1910. Frederick Hall stands at the door of his shop where a useful range of services was available. The main business was plumbing and gas fitting (there is a large gas meter on the front wall), but the firm also embraced the newer technology of electricity. Note the eccentric lettering style sometimes adopted in the early days of electricity.

The Red Cross, Paternoster Square, c. 1910. Jesse Thorn was landlord at the Red Cross pub, which stood in the original Paternoster Square to the north of St Paul's Cathedral. The tiny square had a mixture of shops and commercial premises, and in common with other City squares, there were buildings rather than gardens at its centre. Until the 1860s, Paternoster Square was part of the gruesome Newgate meat market in which animals were slaughtered in the cellars beneath the shops. The incendiary raids of December 1940 left Paternoster Square and its surroundings a fire-blackened ruin, and the little that was left, including the medieval street pattern, was obliterated in the 1960s by the new Paternoster Square with its windswept piazzas, and what the Prince of Wales memorably described as 'a jostling scrum of office buildings'.

The Oxford Arms, off Warwick Lane, from the Old Bailey, c. 1875. Many coaching inns in the City and Southwark were characterized by their wooden galleries overlooking a courtyard, where coaches would disgorge their passengers and goods. Other than a fragment of the George, Southwark, all have disappeared and indeed, the Oxford's delapidated state indicated its own imminent demise. The old inn, which had been rebuilt after the Great Fire, closed around 1868, the washing line on the top gallery evidence of its final role as a tenement.

The Golden Axe pub, St Mary Axe, by Bevis Marks, c. 1870. Many of the City's buildings would have looked like this, wooden-framed and overhanging the roadway, before they were destroyed in the Great Fire. The Golden Axe survived the inferno and lingered on to quench Victorian thirsts in this part of the City, but it has long since vanished.

The White Horse, Little Britain, *c.* 1920. A pair of horse brakes drawn, appropriately, by white horses, prepare to depart for a day out, probably to the races. The White Horse pub, with its opulent hanging lamp, stood by tiny Cross Key Square, which was nothing more than a narrow courtyard. Rebuilding has just taken place here, but in a fine example of conservation, the old frontages onto Little Britain have been preserved, including some of the pub's original tiling.

The Old Swan, Swan Lane, by Old Swan Wharf, *c.* 1905. Landlord Thomas Gomm presided over this once busy but now long departed pub where passengers from the boats calling at Old Swan Pier would have added to the clientele. Despite the commercialism of this Thames-side locality, there was still some residential property beside the pub in Edwardian days.

Upper Thames Street, 1926. There was until recent times a distinctly maritime feel to Upper and Lower Thames Street, historic highways which ran behind the river's wharves and warehouses. In distant centuries, the roads ran close to or beside the Thames before the land was gradually reclaimed from what was once a much wider, shallower river. For centuries ships from distant lands brought their cargoes here, and the air was sometimes fragrant with the scents of spices, overlaid with the more insistent aromas of Billingsgate and tangy whiffs from the Thames foreshore at low tide. Circling seagulls added to the impression that the sea might not be far away. It all changed in post-war years as the docks moved downstream and the sites of the warehouses were filled with glittering office complexes. Dual carriageways, in part running in tunnels beneath the new buildings, replaced the old narrow roadways, and now thundering juggernauts make their way along what is the main east-west route through the City. The photograph is from the 1920s, but shows a scene that might have been enacted at any time in London's history. The premises were those of George Harker & Co. Ltd, colonial produce merchants who occupied the block between Swan Lane, left, and the now defunct Old Swan Lane, right. The firm is pictured during its centenary year, having been founded by George Harker in 1826. The company took a great interest in the wellbeing of its employees and it was remarkable for the length of service put in by some of them. A gathering of warehouse staff is seen here, including Mr A. Clark, who at the age of eighty-two had been with the firm for sixty-six years. A group of thirty-eight employees had between them been with Harker's for 1,422 years! The old warehouse has, of course, long gone, and there is a Corporation of London multistorey car park on the site.

Lower Thames Street from London Bridge Approach, 1920. The road was narrow, irregular, and was dominated by the activities of Billingsgate fish market, whose thirsty workers were provided with good cheer by two of the pubs seen here, the Steam Packet Hotel, left, and the King's Head and Mermaid, centre. Their names brought a further breath of the sea to remind us that this was once a busy port, and part of London's original Docklands.

Billingsgate, c. 1903. London's wholesale fish market fronted the Thames where cargoes of fish were unloaded, and Lower Thames Street where they were transferred to wagons for distribution throughout the capital. Such activities have been carried on here for many centuries – a map of Roman London published in 1722 shows Billingsgate as Belini Porta. Here is a typical scene by Custom House where a pair of wagons have been loaded to overflowing.

A Billingsgate fish porter with his special hard hat and smock, which would have been white at the start of the day's work, c. 1910. The fish are being carried into the market from a ship moored on the Thames.

Billingsgate, near Monument Street, *c*. 1930. There is lively activity in the market as barrels and crates of fish are stacked high on wagons, some of which were still horse-drawn in 1930. Part of the Fishmongers' Hall is seen on the left beyond London Bridge Approach. Inspectors appointed by the Fishmongers' Company were responsible for checking the quality of the fish brought to Billingsgate. This colourful (and aromatic) slice of City life ended in 1982 when the fish market moved downstream to Docklands, but the Fishmongers' Hall can still be seen on its historic site.

Petticoat Lane.
Sunday Mornings

Middlesex Street (Petticoat Lane), *c.* 1909. The City meets the East End at Petticoat Lane, where for over 300 years a rip-roaring Sunday street market, arguably the most famous in London, has jammed the streets with bargain-seeking shoppers. Petticoat Lane's name comes from the garments traditionally sold here since the seventeenth century, while earlier still, in an unimaginable rural past, the road was known as Hog Lane. Petticoat Lane was renamed Middlesex Street in 1830, a name which recalls the days when this was the boundary of the City of London and the county of Middlesex. The present boundary is between the City and the London Borough of Tower Hamlets. This part of London has been a traditional home for waves of immigrants displaced by persecution of one kind or another in their homelands. During the late seventeenth century, French Protestant Huguenots settled around Spitalfields and established silk-weaving workshops whose products doubtless found their way into the market. During the nineteenth century, Jewish immigrants from central Europe created Britain's largest Jewish community to the east of Petticoat Lane. The legendary trading skills of the Jewish people stood them in good stead in the rough-and-tumble of the market, and gave the busy streets hereabouts much of their colourful appeal. In more recent years, with the departure of Jewry for leafier suburbs, a new influx of settlers from Bangladesh has changed the area's character once more. The market, however, is still enlivened by its cockney market traders, whose efforts to attract a good crowd make good entertainment. This view is of a typically lively Sunday morning in the market where, remarkably, only one lady can be spotted in the throng. The building on the right by Cobb Street still stands, suitably tarted up for the 1990s.

Wentworth Street from Middlesex Street (Petticoat Lane), *c.* 1925. Many Jewish businesses prospered in Wentworth Street, which, unlike Petticoat Lane, had a week-day market. New and second hand clothing was on offer here, and there were fruit, vegetables and household goods. There was also refreshment for the weary shopper at Joseph Bonn's restaurant, left, whose frontage with its Yiddish shop sign can be seen on the Petticoat Lane corner.

Wentworth Street, *c.* 1920. The busy market was supplemented by its shops. Those on the right were the emporia of Simon Lewis, oil man, Hyman Cohen, kosher butcher, and Simon Goldberg, draper. Wentworth Street once narrowed considerably by Old Castle Street, in the centre of the picture, where patriotic posters left over from the peace celebrations of 1919 can be seen on the walls of Joseph Palkowski's china shop.

Middlesex Street (Petticoat Lane), *c.* 1910. The buildings along Petticoat Lane have changed through the twentieth century, especially on the City side, left, where the Corporation of London's Middlesex Street Estate has replaced old shops, the Horns pub, and a maze of gloomy byways like Ellison Street. Middlesex Street Estate's Petticoat Tower and Petticoat Square have revived this historic name as an address.

A record stall in Petticoat Lane market, *c.* 1905. A clockwork-driven phonograph and the new Edison Bell gold-moulded wax cylinder records play the musical hits of the day for the entertainment of, and hopeful sale to, the all-male crowd that has gathered round. In the days before electronic amplification, 'loudness' of the records was an important selling point. Disc gramophone records would soon overtake the old cylinders in popularity.

Four

St Paul's Cathedral and the Churches

St Paul's Cathedral, *c*. 1930. There has been a St Paul's Cathedral on the City's high ground since the year 604, but of course the building we know today is of much more recent date. The cathedrals of the first millennium were succeeded by a great Norman building begun in 1087. Further rebuilding during the thirteenth century resulted in a mighty Gothic structure with a spire that reached 489 ft above street level. 'Old' St Paul's was all but destroyed in the Great Fire although services continued for a while amid the tottering ruins of the nave. Sir Christopher Wren was given the task of designing a new St Paul's, the first stone of which was laid on 21 June 1675. The building was finished in 1711 and London had a fine new Baroque cathedral, a building which was later held in such affection that it was referred to as 'the parish church of the nation'. The cathedral overlooked the City as it rose from the ashes of the Fire with new brick buildings and Wren churches to replace the ancient City churches that succumbed to the flames. A second great conflagration, the air raids of the Second World War, once again changed the landscape around the cathedral, whose massive dome became a symbol of Britain's defiance in a time of adversity as the City blazed around it. This pre-war view shows the densely built-up streets still following the medieval street pattern to the north of the cathedral before they were turned into the vast bomb sites of Paternoster Row and Ivy Lane and, in the 1960s, the grimly soulless acres of the new Paternoster Square.

Old St Paul's in a drawing from around 1560. The old cathedral was a vast Gothic wonder, its height emphasized by its elevated site on the highest hill in the City. As St Paul's was added to through the centuries, it eventually swallowed up the site of another church, St Faith's, whose congregation was then accommodated in a part of the cathedral crypt thenceforward known as 'St Faith's-under-St Paul's'. In 1666, Sir Christopher Wren submitted plans to the Dean of St Paul's for a dome to replace the spire which had been destroyed during a thunderstorm in 1561, but within days the cathedral had been burnt out in the Great Fire.

St Paul's and Foster Lane from Gresham Street, c. 1911. The massive proportions of the cathedral ensured its dominating presence on the City skyline. Demolition of old buildings would sometimes open out a new view of it, as here when the eastern block of GPO buildings in St Martin's-le-Grand was removed. To the left is the hall of the Goldsmiths' Company, one of the wealthiest of the City Livery Companies. The hall dates from 1829-35. (© Judges Postcards, Hastings)

St Paul's from Cannon Street, c. 1920. This is now the most popular viewpoint for the cathedral following the removal of the buildings which once crowded in upon it. There are now gardens in place of the office block to the right, and a new street called New Change has replaced its predecessor, Old Change, from which we see a Corporation of London water tanker emerging.

St Paul's Churchyard from the cathedral, *c.* 1908. These were the buildings which restricted the view of St Paul's from Cannon Street until their wartime destruction gave the opportunity to create the grand view we know today. On the Old Change corner, left, was the church of St Augustine, Watling Street, a church of twelfth-century origin rebuilt by Wren in 1683, and wrecked during an air raid on 11 January 1941. Its tower survived and now forms part of St Paul's Cathedral Choir School. Much of what can be seen here has been replaced by gardens including a wall fountain, the gift of the Worshipful Company of Gardeners in 1951.

St Paul's Churchyard, *c.* 1920. The northern part of St Paul's Churchyard was once a considerable shopping area, with department stores and smaller shops. Most of the buildings survived the war but were demolished later to make way for the Paternoster Square scheme of 1961-7. The sole survivor is Wren's Chapter House of 1712-14, left, which, although burnt out, has been beautifully restored.

St Paul's from Watling Street, *c.* 1930. A walk through the City will often reveal a surprise view of St Paul's filling the skyline at the end of a narrow byway. Here, ancient Watling Street is seen before the war stripped it of many of its old buildings, some of whose sites were used for the construction of a modern road, New Change. The Wren church of St Augustine can be seen in the centre beyond Friday Street, its spire dwarfed by the cathedral behind it. Friday Street derives its name from the fish market held there on Fridays during the twelfth century while Bread Street, on the left, was named after the bakers who once traded there. (© Judges Postcards, Hastings)

St Bartholomew-the-Great, West Smithfield, c. 1903. One of the most beautiful of the ancient City churches, St Bartholomew-the-Great already had a history spanning eight centuries when this image was produced. Beneath a seventeenth-century brick tower, the church's venerable stonework bears evidence of its foundation in 1123 as an Augustinian monastery by Rahere, a courtier of Henry I. Much of St Bartholomew's was demolished at the time of the Dissolution of the Monasteries under Henry VIII, but the choir was allowed to remain as a place of worship for local people. A fragment of ancient wall, on the right, was once part of the nave which was large enough to cover everything pictured here.

The Gatehouse, St Bartholomew-the-Great, c. 1950. The thirteenth-century stone arch beneath the Gatehouse was the street entrance to the nave from West Smithfield; the house above was built in 1559. The house was 'modernized' with a brick front when Tudor architecture became unfashionable, but with the assistance of the First World War bomb which partly exposed the timber work, the house was restored as we see it here.

St James's Garlickhythe in 1800 and 1900. This is a twelfth-century church, rebuilt by Wren between 1676 and 1682 and severely damaged by wartime bombing. The church narrowly escaped total destruction when a 500 lb bomb lodged in its stonework failed to explode. A fine post-war restoration revived St James's former beauty, but a falling crane from a building site inflicted further damage in 1991, now happily repaired. The church stands in Garlick Hill, which was named after the produce once traded here. The pair of views shows how commercial buildings encroached upon the church during the nineteenth century.

St James's Garlickhythe from Upper Thames Street, January 1941. The debris of war litters Garlick Hill, the church railings are thrown about and the tower clock destroyed. Post-war alterations have removed the remains of the buildings on the right in the foreground, revealing the south side of the church and giving it a new setting beside Upper Thames Street from where it makes a fine sight. The church clock was restored in 1988.

Love Lane (Lovat Lane) and St Mary-at-Hill from Eastcheap, c. 1905. This narrow, cobbled lane plunges steeply downhill towards Billingsgate, passing St Mary-at-Hill, another Wren rebuilding (with a later tower dating from 1787) of a twelfth-century church. Love Lane was called Rope Lane in the thirteenth century after the rope makers who worked here; the modern name, Lovat Lane, was adopted to avoid confusion with the City's other Love Lane off Aldermanbury.

St Magnus the Martyr, Lower Thames Street, *c.* 1905. Building started on this Wren church in 1671, and provided a covered footpath beneath the church tower as an approach to old London Bridge. Here we see the beautifully designed tower rising above the gridlocked traffic of Edwardian Billingsgate. The church now has some eye-catching new neighbours in place of the Bell pub and the dingy warehouses of old.

St Alphege's Churchyard, London Wall, *c.* 1910. St Alphege's was founded in the eleventh century and closed in 1924, but a fine length of Roman wall, part of a fort dating from around 120 AD, can still be seen in its former churchyard. The Roman remains made a solid base for the Victorian office buildings constructed on top of them. These have now gone and the wall is free-standing once more. Remains of the church's fourteenth-century tower are to be found close by in London Wall.

St Giles' Cripplegate from Fore Street, 1930. There was a church on this site from 1090, but a rebuilding of 1390 forms the basis of the church we know today. St Giles' underwent many alterations through the centuries, but the Great Fire spared it. The church where William Shakespeare worshipped and Oliver Cromwell married was struck on 24 August 1940 by the first bomb to fall on a City church during the Second World War. An incendiary bomb on 29 December 1940 gutted the church, and by the end of the war, St Giles' battered tower looked out over a nightmare landscape of seemingly endless bomb sites, and Fore Street had almost ceased to exist. Following restoration, St Giles' became the parish church of the vast Barbican development, within which it now stands.

St Mary-le-Bow, Cheapside, *c.* 1920. One of Wren's grandest church designs, St Mary-le-Bow stands above an eleventh-century crypt on the remains of a Roman road. The church was severely damaged by the war, but was rebuilt by Laurence King between 1956 and 1964 following Wren's design. The church bells, Bow-bells, are held in particular affection by Londoners who insist that to be a true Cockney one must be born within their sound. Cheapside evolved from the West Cheap and was from the eleventh century or earlier the 'High Street' of the City, and its principal market place. Ironmonger Lane, right, is yet another street name to remind us of the City's twelfth-century traders.

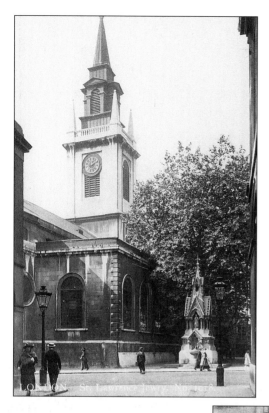

St Lawrence Jewry, Gresham Street, from Guildhall Buildings (Guildhall Yard), c. 1920. This twelfth-century church was so named because of its proximity to a Jewish quarter of the City. The church was burnt out in the Great Fire, a fate also suffered by its Wren replacement during the war, but the restored church opened again in 1957. The opulent Gothic drinking fountain was put up in 1866 but removed in 1972.

Falcon Square Chapel, c. 1898. The City's treasury of historic churches was complemented by a number of other places of worship, including this little classically fronted independent chapel in Falcon Square. The narrowness of the chapel's frontage, sandwiched between the Falcon pub on the left and Levy Lewis's hairdressers saloon on the right, was an indication of how congested this part of the City once was. Falcon Square was tiny, with only twenty-seven buildings, and was surrounded by a dense network of narrow alleys and back streets. It lay close to what is now the post-war extension of London Wall by Aldersgate Street near the Museum of London, but no trace of the square or its chapel remains today.

Five
City Celebrations

The Diamond Jubilee, Bank of England, June 1897. Great royal events are celebrated with enthusiasm in the City, as shown here with decorated buildings for the Queen Victoria's Diamond Jubilee. The Bank of England, left, and the Royal Exchange, right, show very early examples of electric illuminations including the V R (for 'Victoria Regina'), which had been set with electric bulbs on the flower-garlanded columns of the Royal Exchange. The white boards to the right concealed the construction site of Bank station.

The Diamond Jubilee, June 1897. Protected from a hot summer sun by a white parasol, Queen Victoria acknowledges the cheers of the City as her carriage and a grand procession passes along Cheapside and Poultry. The Queen attended a Diamond Jubilee service at St Paul's, held at the bottom of the cathedral steps so that the increasingly frail monarch could remain in her carriage throughout.

Coronation decorations, London Bridge, August 1902. A new century soon brought a new monarch, and the City celebrated with the nation as King Edward VII and Queen Alexandra were crowned in Westminster Abbey. London Bridge was decked out with floral garlands during coronation week.

Coronation decorations, Royal Exchange, August 1902. An amateur photographer's snapshot captures the mood as London prepares to celebrates the first coronation for sixty-five years and the beginning of the Edwardian era. For those with a head for heights, the stands erected on the roof of the Royal Exchange would have given a panoramic, if distant, view of the coronation procession.

Coronation Arch, London Bridge, June 1911. King Edward's reign was a short one and on 22 June 1911 it was time to celebrate another coronation, that of King George V and Queen Mary. The City Corporation put up this flamboyant arch at London Bridge, from where a royal procession set off through London on the day after coronation day. Special stands had been erected for spectators by Fishmonger's Hall on the left.

The coronation procession on 23 June 1911, seen from the Southwark side of London Bridge, showing the Monument and church of St Magnus the Martyr. The royal procession, led by military bands, sets off from London Bridge.

Coronation Arch, Temple Bar, Fleet Street, June 1911. Crowds are beginning to gather to view the procession at the boundaries of the Cities of London and Westminster on the historic route between the two cities.

Royal procession, 23 June 1911. Their Majesties' carriage passes by Temple Bar and the Law Courts, beneath a banner bearing the City arms. In the background, intrepid spectators have climbed onto the roof of St Clement Danes church for a better view.

Fleet Street, May 1935. The *Daily Telegraph*'s clock looks down on a Fleet Street where the familiar landmarks have all but disappeared behind a colourful display of patriotism. The occasion was the Silver Jubilee of King George V and Queen Mary for which a service of thanksgiving was held at St Paul's Cathedral.

Fleet Street from Ludgate Circus, May 1935. Fleet Street would be closed to allow the royal procession through, but meanwhile there were newspapers to produce with special editions full of the latest royal news.

Ludgate Hill and St Paul's Cathedral, May 1935. Amid the splendour of the Jubilee decorations, the life of the City goes on and a traffic jam builds up on Ludgate Hill. In the foreground of this view is the site of Lud Gate, an entry point in the City wall, removed in 1760.

The Lord Mayor's State Coach, Guildhall Yard, *c.* 1906. Londoners have a chance to see the magnificent State Coach every year as it conveys the Lord Mayor of London through the City's streets during the Lord Mayor's Show. For the rest of the year it is on permanent exhibition at the Museum of London in the Barbican. The coach was built in 1757, and is seen here with the Lord Mayor's coachman in his eighteenth-century livery, and one of the liveried Walking Footmen who accompany the coach on foot during processions.

Guildhall, *c.* 1903. The Lord Mayor's semi-state coach waits by Guildhall, the City's civic and administrative heart. Guildhall dates from 1411 and its frontage from 1788, part of which is missing here as a result of a Victorian scheme to restore its medieval appearance. The frontage was replaced in 1910 uniting the two halves of the façade once more (see p. 117).

City of London Police, c. 1911. The City is unique in that it has its own police force; the Metropolitan Police protect the rest of London. The City Police are easily distinguished from their Metropolitan counterparts by their Roman-style helmets which carry the City crest. These mounted officers were pictured near Guildhall, possibly in readiness for a Lord Mayor's Show.

Yeoman Warders, Tower of London, c. 1910. The Yeoman Warders are seen here in their scarlet and gold full dress uniforms carrying their halberds, a combination of battleaxe and spear. Among the ancient ceremonies of the Tower of London is the daily Ceremony of the Keys, which has taken place for the last 700 years.

Blackfriars, 1903. More street decorations, this time in honour of the visit of President Loubet of France. This country's friendly relationship with France in Edwardian times culminated in the establishment of an 'Entente Cordiale' between the two nations in 1904. Franco-British friendship led further to a great exhibition in 1908 at the then new White City near Shepherds Bush. The Moorish architecture of old Blackfriars station has given this City street scene an almost Middle Eastern appearance, despite a sight of St Paul's in the background.

St Paul's Cathedral, 6 July 1919. The nightmare years of the First World War had finally ended and it was time for the nation to give thanks for the peace that came at last. A service attended by King George V, Queen Mary and the Royal Family was held on the steps of St Paul's.

Six

City Transport

The City of London, with neighbouring Westminster, is the focus of a complex transport system, the foundations of which were laid in the nineteenth century. The first railway arrived in London in 1836 and in 1841 the first station in the City, Fenchurch Street, was opened by the London & Blackwall Railway. The Metropolitan railway was the first underground railway in the world with a line from Paddington to Farringdon Street. Deep level electric 'Tubes' appeared in 1890 when the City and South London line to King William Street opened. London's first bus service, a route from Marylebone to Bank, began in 1829; it proved popular, and was joined by a host of other routes. Regular horse tram services made their debut in the 1870s, followed by electric trams which ran at the edge of the City but never through the narrow streets at its heart. Motor buses made a noisy appearance in Edwardian times, and with increasing mechanical sophistication, ousted the old horse buses. Cabs for the more affluent were similarly motorized. The Bank of England is the location of this picture from around 1912, when four types of City transport have come together: a motor cab, motor bus, a horse bus, and the Underground at Bank station on the right. The motor bus was working London's most famous route, the 11, which has been running past many of the capital's notable landmarks for over ninety years.

Horse tram, *c.* 1886. The first trams to serve the City of London were horse-drawn, and were operated from the early 1870s by the North Metropolitan Tramways Company. This picturesque tramcar, one of London's earliest, ran from Clapton Pond to a terminus at the City boundary in Aldersgate Street, by Fann Street (see p. 86).

Moorgate Street tram terminus, Finsbury Pavement, *c.* 1903. The trams here were introduced in 1871 and brought the City's workers and shoppers in from London's northern suburbs; the tram shown here had just arrived from Highgate. Moorgate Street's horse trams had a long life span which lasted until March 1907 when smart new electric trams made their appearance.

The tram terminus, Victoria Embankment, *c. 1907*. The longest stretch of tramway in the City was powered by electricity from the outset, and ran along Victoria Embankment from Blackfriars towards Westminster. This photograph shows a temporary terminus of the line located just short of Blackfriars Bridge – it would not be until 14 September 1909 that the specially widened bridge could accommodate the trams and the line could be completed. The new tracks soon proved a valuable link in the London tramway system, connecting the west of the City with the vast South London tramway network, and via the Kingsway tram subway, the northern suburbs. A casualty of the new line was the cab rank which was displaced in favour of the trams. One of the characteristic wooden shelters for cab drivers is visible in the background. Many people will remember the Embankment trams, which gave their top-deck passengers a series of splendid views of the river and its bridges glimpsed through the trees. The last trams in London ran here on the night of 5/6 July 1952 at the end of 'Last Tram Week', when Londoners said a nostalgic goodbye to a form of transportation that had served the capital well for around eighty years. The scene here has been transformed by the building of Blackfriars Underpass (opened 26 July 1967), but the Embankment still retains its famous 'camel' seats, one of which is seen on the right.

Blackfriars tram station, Victoria Embankment, *c.* 1920. The continuous streams of trams arriving from all parts of London had the rare luxury here of a reserved track for their exclusive use, and passengers could wait for their tram in a large, covered shelter. This was built in 1911 and came equipped with an early public address system which Londoners, never short of an appropriate word, called the 'tramophone'.

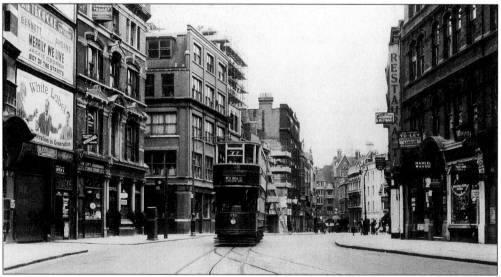

Aldersgate Street tram terminus from Goswell Road, *c.* 1938. Withdrawal of North London's trams in favour of trolleybuses began in the 1930s, a process halted by the outbreak of war. Route number 77 to West India Docks was seen for the last time on 10 September 1939, and was replaced by trolleybus route 677 which terminated at nearby Smithfield. To the left of the tram is Fann Street, which in post-war years would separate the City Corporation's Golden Lane housing estate (built 1953-62) from the mighty Barbican which was begun in 1963. The view today is dominated by the Barbican YMCA building, and Lauderdale Tower, one of the Barbican's trio of residential tower blocks which stand over 400 ft tall and were the tallest blocks of flats in Europe when first built.

City (Southwark Bridge) tram terminus, Queen Street Place, *c.* 1937. City commuters, their day's work over, climb aboard a tram bound for residential Denmark Hill and Dulwich. The line which carried the trams across Southwark Bridge and a few yards into the City just short of Upper Thames Street was a late-comer in the tramway system, not arriving until July 1925. The last trams here ran on the night of 6/7 October 1951. The background shows the Kings Head pub by Queen Street, whose site, along with those of adjacent buildings, now lies beneath the dual carriageway of the widened Upper Thames Street. Queen Street has been pedestrianized at that point, but Thames House (left), an office block dating from 1911, still stands. Queen Street was one of the new City roads laid out after the Great Fire. (Tony Davies, Marylebone Gallery)

A trolleybus, *c.* 1959. Although trams did not pollute the atmosphere, they were noisy and shook the ground as they passed by, whereas trolleybuses were swift, silent and comfortable. They replaced trams at several points around the City and shared a terminus at Minories with Green Line coaches and buses. The trolleybus shown here was built at the end of the 1930s and is seen emerging from the Minories terminus into Aldgate High Street. London's trolleybuses lasted for just over thirty years – the last one ran in May 1962.

Farringdon station, May 1933. This is an original section of the world's first underground passenger railway, the Metropolitan, which opened on 10 January 1863. At first, the Metropolitan railway ran from Paddington to Farringdon Street, and from 23 December 1865 was extended to Aldersgate Street station (now Barbican) and beyond. These early lines ran in part through shallow cuttings as seen here, with Turnmill Street on the left and St Paul's on the horizon. The first station at Farringdon was built of wood and was located by Farringdon Street (now Farringdon Road) to the right of the picture, beyond the sidings. The existing Farringdon station is a grade II listed building dating from 1923. (R.W. Kidner)

Outside Aldgate station, *c.* 1903. A steam train on the Inner Circle is reminiscent of the days when the older sections of the Underground were characterized by their soot-blackened walls, even though the locomotives were specially designed to contain the worst of their emissions. Smoke was a considerable nuisance in the subterranean stations and tunnels until electrification could be completed.

Aldgate station, Aldgate High Street, *c.* 1912. This Metropolitan railway station opened on 18 November 1876 and was rebuilt in 1926 with its now familiar white tiled frontage. Aldgate was another busy transport interchange, with numerous bus and tram routes nearby. The church of St Botolph, Aldgate, is seen rising above a vanished landmark, the Three Nuns Hotel. This was built in 1876, having originated as a seventeenth-century coaching inn.

Liverpool Street, c. 1920. This railway-dominated street had three stations, all of which are visible here. Liverpool Street Underground station, at the centre, opened in 1875 as 'Bishopsgate' and was given its present name in 1909; by 1912 there were four Underground lines using it. Liverpool Street station, centre right, was the London terminus of the Great Eastern Railway and opened in 1875. Broad Street station (with the scaffolding) was the City terminus of the North London Railway and opened in 1865. Its demolition in 1985 preceded the development of the remarkable Broadgate, a stylish office, shopping and leisure complex with an outdoor skating rink.

Mark Lane station, c. 1912. Although its entrance can still be recognized, one might search in vain for Mark Lane station on an Underground map following its renaming as Tower Hill on 1 September 1946 and closure on 4 February 1967. A new Tower Hill station took over its duties, its site being that of the short-lived Tower of London station which had opened in 1882. The old Mark Lane station entrance was in Byward Street near Seething Lane.

Bank Station, *c*. 1901. At the end of the nineteenth century most of London's Underground travellers had to endure the vapours of its steam-hauled trains, but the pioneering City and South London Railway (now the Northern Line) gave the capital a taste of the future with the world's first electric Tube, which opened on 18 December 1890 between Stockwell and King William Street. The line was extended to Bank on 25 February 1900, and was joined there on 30 July 1900 by the Central London Railway running from Shepherds Bush. The photograph of one of the Central platforms at Bank shows an impressive gathering of station staff, but the wooden platforms and woodwork along the tracks would be an unacceptable fire risk today.

The booking office at Bank station, *c*. 1903. Everyone pauses in their activities for the photographer at the only station on the original section of the Central London Railway not to have a booking hall at street level. A flat fare of 2d led to the line's nickname of 'Twopenny Tube'.

Post Office station, *c.* 1903. The distinctive style of the Central stations with their terra-cotta stonework is well demonstrated here. The station was so named because of its proximity to the General Post Office buildings in St Martin's-le-Grand, but following several rebuildings and resitings, we know it now as St Paul's, the name it took on 1 February 1937.

Chancery Lane station, *c.* 1904. The original entrance to Chancery Lane station was on the north side of High Holborn, but it was rendered redundant from 25 June 1934 when a new sub-surface booking hall was opened with entrances by Gray's Inn Road and Staple Inn. Although heavily disguised by paint and shop fronts, the old entrance can still be spotted today.

92

Temporary bridge at Bank station, 1941. One of the City's great wartime tragedies occurred on the night of 11/12 January 1941, when Bank station was struck by a bomb which caused the roadway to collapse into the booking hall killing thirty-five people. The loss of the road at this busy multiple junction caused additional chaos, but on 3 February 1941, the Lord Mayor of London opened a temporary bridge over what became known as 'the largest crater in London'. The road was soon rebuilt and opened for normal use. The Royal Exchange is in the background with a banner bearing the wartime slogan 'Dig for Victory'.

Ludgate Hill station from Ludgate Circus, c. 1908. One of the City's 'lost' stations, Ludgate Hill was built by the London, Chatham and Dover Railway in 1865, and presented an imposing frontage to New Bridge Street until closure in 1929. The station was then hidden away behind a row of shops until 1990, when demolition of the shops briefly revealed the old station before it too was pulled down. A new station in Ludgate Hill itself now takes Thameslink services.

Fenchurch Street station, *c*. 1910. Fenchurch Street was the first station in the City and dates from 1841. It was the terminus of the London and Blackwall Railway, whose trains were hauled by cable from Blackwall to Minories station. The trains were then 'thrown off' the cable at Minories, and reached Fenchurch Street by the momentum thus attained. The trains returned to Minories down a slight slope, with gravity helped by a push from the station staff. This bizarre practice ended in 1849 when steam trains took over.

Fenchurch Street station, John Street (Crosswall), 1910. A new Fenchurch Street station was built in 1854. It is impressive enough at the front, but this view of the back entrance in John Street (now Crosswall) tells another story. For many years, the station was used by the London, Tilbury and Southend Railway, and the Great Eastern Railway. The poster advertising a 9d return fare to Chingford looks tempting. This site is now occupied by No. 1 America Square, one of the City's exciting new wave of 1990s office buildings.

Liverpool Street station from Old Broad Street, *c*. 1904. The Great Eastern Railway created its City terminus here in 1875 on part of the site of what was from 1246 to 1676 the Hospital of St Mary of Bethlehem, or Bethlem, an asylum for the insane from which the word 'Bedlam' originated. The station was one of London's busiest with eighteen platforms taking suburban and main line services. The Gothic building on the right survives.

The concourse, Liverpool Street station, *c*. 1910. The station survived post-war threats of total redevelopment and was remodelled to create a most agreeable environment: light, airy and full of shops on two levels, and with the best of the original architecture carefully restored. This view is of the old concourse with its wrought ironwork, soot-blackened since Victorian times by the belchings of countless steam-engines.

Buses at the Bank, *c.* 1908. A cross-section of Edwardian road transport at this busy multiple junction includes cabs, horse buses, motor buses and, centre, a bus powered by electric batteries. These environmentally-friendly vehicles ran from 1906 to 1910 and were owned by the London Electrobus Company of Victoria. They had a range of some twenty miles, but had to then return to their depot for a battery recharge.

Traffic at the Bank, *c.* 1912. The bus is operating route 33, and is an example of London's first standardized type, the 'B', of which around 3,000 entered service, replacing horse buses and earlier motor buses. They were introduced in 1910 and operated by the London General Omnibus Company, forerunners of London Transport.

'B' type bus at St Paul's Churchyard, *c*. 1920. These buses ran throughout the First World War, but their numbers were depleted when over 900 of them were shipped to the continent to act as troop transport, or were used for other war work in this country. The varied architecture of the buildings on the right by Ludgate Hill is in marked contrast to the plain buildings put up here in the 1960s.

Buses in Bishopsgate, by Liverpool Street, *c*. 1920. Passengers crowd aboard a Leyton-bound 'B' type bus at this lively transport interchange with its railway and tram termini. The fruit seller on the left with his banana-laden barrow should have had a good day.

The General Strike, May 1926. For nine days during May 1926, Britain was paralysed by a strike of transport workers, dockers, railwaymen and industrial workers. Normal transportation ceased in London, but an emergency bus service of sorts was provided by civilian drivers and conductors using an assortment of often elderly vehicles working a few makeshift routes. The strike breakers attracted inevitable hostility from those still refusing to work, and it was often necessary for a police constable to sit beside the driver in his exposed position to deal with any trouble. This was obviously not needed on this bus, which has been fortified with planks over its windows and a wire netting grille to protect the driver from anything thrown at him during his journey from Victoria to Liverpool Street. Note the crudely chalked route details on the front of the bus, which was photographed at St Paul's Churchyard. This bus also played a part in another colourful period in the capital's transport history and, indeed, began life by flouting the accepted rules, as it does here. Most of London's bus routes were operated by the London General Omnibus Company, but from 1922 a new breed of independent or 'pirate' bus operators took to the streets and entered into fierce competition with General and each other for the fare-paying passengers. It all degenerated into a free-for-all as buses tore about the streets in an effort to clear a bus stop of passengers before their rivals. This bus was one of nine owned by the Gray family of Stamford Hill. In time, the 'pirates' declined and by the time London Transport was created in 1933, they had almost disappeared. (Tony Davies, Marylebone Gallery)

Seven
A City Miscellany

Paternoster Row from St Paul's Churchyard, *c*. 1920. This ancient thoroughfare was once inhabited by mercers, haberdashers and the sellers of 'Paternosters' or prayer beads. Samuel Pepys and his wife found the street's fashionable shops greatly to their taste. The Great Fire destroyed it all, but the rebuilt Paternoster Row became a base for many of the City's booksellers and publishers. In a return to earlier days, mercers and drapers Nicholson's Ltd set up their business here in 1843 and rebuilt their premises in 1900. Paternoster Row was all but destroyed during the air raids of 29 December 1940 when the booksellers and publishers lost around six million volumes. Nicholson's continued trading until 1965, when closure was followed by demolition and development of the site as part of the Paternoster Square scheme. This photograph preserves an evocative slice of City street life from the 1920s, with two gentlemen finding time for a smoke and a chat on the right, while a flower girl in a white apron tempts Nicholson's lady shoppers with her blossoms, on the left. The contrast with the Paternoster Row of today, a sunken service road for Paternoster Square's grim office blocks, could not be greater.

Ivy Lane by Dukes Head Passage, *c.* 1935. This narrow street of medieval origin ran from Paternoster Row to Newgate Street, and was filled with a typical City mixture of shops, pubs and offices until it was obliterated by the air raids of December 1940. The view looks south towards St Paul's Cathedral, one of whose towers is seen above the rooftops. Anyone standing at this point today would see a grand view of St Paul's but would be surrounded by the desolate emptiness of the partly abandoned Paternoster Square piazza. The photograph reminds us of how tranquil the City can be on a Sunday when the shops and offices are closed.

Ave Maria Lane, 1940. The air raid of 29 December 1940, which destroyed Paternoster Row, also left Ave Maria Lane a fire-blackened ruin. The stark concrete walls of post-war rebuilding predominate here now, but further along by Warwick Lane and Amen Corner, the seventeenth-century Amen Court has survived. Another precious survival is the partly seventeenth-century hall of the Stationers' Company, approached via a passageway to the left.

Jewry Street, 1941. This little building was erected in 1650 just before one disaster, the Great Fire, and is seen here surrounded by rubble of another one, the Second World War. The shop was run by J. Sly & Son who sold ropes, tackle and sacks. The shop window was reduced in size as was usual during the war, but the old building with its picturesque weatherboarded rear elevation was later pulled down.

Godliman Street, August 1939. These are not more views of the Blitz, but a bizarre foretaste of the sort of scene that was soon to become all too familiar. The culprit here was a broken water main which undermined a gas main, causing a massive explosion which destroyed buildings in Knightrider Street, left. The humour of the Londoner in times of adversity has been caught here with a notice in the hairdresser's window, right, informing clients that 'George' had been 'blown to 59a Carter Lane' where he doubtless continued to provide his 4d shaves and 8d haircuts. A knot of people are standing by Bakehouse Yard, from where St Paul's Bakehouse once supplied bread to St Paul's Cathedral. The girder framework of a new extension to Faraday House is seen beyond Knightrider Street.

Knightrider Street from Sermon Lane, August 1939. The total destruction of buildings in Knightrider Street beyond Godliman Street is shown well here. The gas explosion shattered windows over a wide area, including some in St Paul's Cathedral, the College of Arms and St Benet's church. Some twenty-one tons of broken plate glass were cleared by the City's cleansing department.

The Monument, *c.* 1920. On the night of 1/2 September 1666, a small fire began in Thomas Faryner's bakery in Pudding Lane near Billingsgate. With combustible materials lying around, the fire took hold and, driven by a brisk east wind, began to consume the City's wooden houses and warehouses at an alarming rate. Thus began the Great Fire of London, the worst disaster in the City's history. By the time it had burnt itself out on 7 September, much of the City and most of its landmarks were in ruins. Architect Sir Christopher Wren accepted the task of designing a new City and a Monument to the calamity that had destroyed the old one. The Monument was built between 1671 and 1677 and at 202 ft from the ground to the gilded flames that crown it, it is the world's tallest isolated stone column. Its scale may be judged by the tiny figures seen on the viewing gallery, reached via 311 exhausting steps.

Whitefriars fire station, Carmelite Street, *c.* 1910. At the time of the Great Fire, the meagre fire-fighting resources were the responsibility of local parishes. During the following centuries, insurance companies organised their own brigades, and by 1833 a London-wide brigade had been formed. This was taken over by the London County Council in 1889, and became known as the London Fire Brigade from 1904. Whitefriars fire station, whose foundation stone was laid on 19 March 1896, was one of the Gothic-style buildings favoured by the LCC and was erected in Carmelite Street, one of the new roads laid out over the site of the old City of London gasworks (see pp. 38-9). This impressive Whitefriars 'turn-out' is from a time when the traditional horse-drawn appliances were being replaced by powerful new motor fire engines. Although closed now, the old building can still be recognized in its new role as an office block. To the left of the photograph was another of the new roads on the gasworks site, which was named after Thomas Tallis, the English composer of church music. The Whitefriars, Blackfriars and Carmelite names hereabouts all recall the ancient monastic establishments of this part of the City.

Queen Victoria Street from New Bridge Street, *c.* 1920. Queen Victoria Street was created between 1867 and 1871 as a continuation of the Embankment scheme to link Westminster with the Bank of England. As with the Embankment, the new District Underground line was built beneath it. Our view is still recognizable, with the Black Friar pub (1875) on its triangular site by Blackfriars Court. Long gone, however, are the City Corporation's steam-driven wagons on the right, and the railway bridge has been slimmed down.

The Times building, Queen Victoria Street, *c.* 1920. The handsomely pedimented *Times* building backed onto Printing House Square from where *The Times* was produced (originally as the *Daily Universal Register*) from 1785. The premises were rebuilt during the 1960s, but the newspaper moved away from the City in 1974. The Wren church of St Andrew-by-the-Wardrobe is seen in the centre, with the Baynard Castle pub in front of it. The pub's name comes from the Thames-side castle which stood from Norman times until the Great Fire. The City's first permanent theatre for 300 years, the Mermaid, was opened at nearby Puddle Dock in 1959. The steps once led down to Upper Thames Street, but a complex modern road system predominates now.

Wardrobe Place, c. 1920. Among the delights of the City are its hidden corners where there are still tantalizing reminders of how much of it once looked. Wardrobe Place, off Carter Lane, retains typical houses from the post-fire rebuilding of the City – these ones date from around 1710. The 'Wardrobe' names here come from the King's Wardrobe, the building in which the royal state robes were kept until it was destroyed in the Great Fire.

St Paul's and Benet's Hill from Paul's Pier Wharf. A narrow gas-lit lane running between sooty warehouse walls – not a Victorian photograph, but one taken by the author as recently as the 1960s. It is all unrecognizable now, with only the cathedral and the Guild Church of St Benet, Paul's Wharf, whose corner wall is seen by Upper Thames Street, still with us. The new buildings of St Paul's School, whose foundation stone was laid on 24 May 1985, cover much of what we see here. Close by, St Paul's Vista, a new partly stepped street created out of old Peter's Hill, climbs steeply towards St Paul's Cathedral.

The Bank of England, c. 1902. The Bank of England was founded in 1694 and has stood here in Threadneedle Street since 1732. This was originally the site of the home of its first governor, Sir John Houblon. Extensions to the Bank between 1766 and 1786 swallowed up the church of St Christopher-le-Stocks and from 1788 work began on a further rebuilding by Sir John Soane.

The Bank of England, c. 1932. Sir John Soane's Bank was a structure mostly only one storey high, which somewhat wasteful of its prime City site, but another building programme from 1925 to 1939 within Soane's preserved outer walls gave the Bank much-needed extra floor space. The loss of Soane's much admired Bank was mourned by many, but the new buildings, seen from a similar point to the top photograph, were a handsome addition to the City scene. (© Judges Postcards, Hastings)

The Royal Exchange, *c*. 1920. The first Royal Exchange, a meeting place for City merchants to conduct their business, was opened in 1566 and the present building, the third on the site, was opened by Queen Victoria in 1844. The building's classical columns look down on the busy forecourt, itself something of a meeting place away from the constant traffic. Note the old-style Underground map on the left; this predates the geometric design so familiar today. The buildings in Cornhill, right, would soon suffer a bizarre fate; see p. 110.

The Royal Exchange and Bank of England, *c*. 1908. The photograph is called 'A Wet Day in the City', and indeed it was a particularly wretched one, with only umbrellas for protection on the old open-topped buses.

'The Cornhill Crash', 6 August 1927. The crowds turn out to view the spectacle as part of the Commercial Union Assurance building collapses into an excavation being prepared for a new Lloyds Bank next door. Having overcome this mishap, the new bank was ready for occupation by 1929.

110

Leadenhall Street, c. 1920. The site of this forbidding Victorian block is now occupied by one of the City's most remarkable post-war buildings, the possibly shocking but always exciting Lloyd's of London. Lloyd's, with its exposed piping and ductwork, was designed by Sir Richard Rogers and built in the early 1980s. It is the latest manifestation of a City institution that began in the 1680s as Lloyd's Coffee House in Tower Street, where those concerned with maritime matters gathered to obtain shipping news and, later, to seek marine insurance.

King William Street and Eastcheap, c. 1920. By City standards, King William Street has a short history, being laid out between 1829 and 1835 to allow better access to the then newly rebuilt London Bridge. The statue of William IV was removed to Greenwich in 1935. Eastcheap, at the centre, is much more ancient and from the eleventh century was one of the two principal City markets, the other being Westcheap, the present Cheapside.

111

Love Lane (Lovat Lane), c. 1905. Although much rebuilt, Love Lane (Lovat Lane from 1939), with its cobblestones and central drainage gully, manages to retain much of its old-world City atmosphere as it descends steeply from Eastcheap to Billingsgate. The large house with the steps was the back of a mansion in Botolph Lane once occupied by Sir Christopher Wren. The house was demolished in 1906. To the right, the premises of George Sproston, fish salesman, were conveniently close to Billingsgate market, while next door, there was a 'first class wareroom' (presumably a mini-warehouse) to let.

Seething Lane from Hart Street and Crutched Friars, *c*. 1912. The bonded warehouses, left, covered the site of the Navy Office where Samuel Pepys lived and worked until 1673. This was part of a large site to be cleared for the new Port of London Authority building which was completed in 1922. Seething Lane was transformed by the development which created some welcome greenery in the shape of Seething Lane Gardens (Pepys Garden), and two new streets, Pepys Street and Muscovy Street. Pepys Street runs opposite the partly thirteenth-century St Olave's church, right, which survived the Great Fire but was wrecked during the Blitz and later restored.

Site of Old Catherine Court. E.C
Clearing for New Port of London Authority Buildings

Clearing the site for the Port of London Authority building, Seething Lane, *c*. 1913. This was the first large-scale redevelopment of the City during the twentieth century, and it swallowed up most of an area of warehouses and streets bounded by Seething Lane, Crutched Friars, Savage Gardens and Trinity Square. Although few were sorry to see the end of the warehouses, many regretted the loss of Catherine Court, a charming gated close of elegant houses dating from 1720. The last of Catherine Court's houses are seen to the right in a partly demolished state. Also lost was Muscovy Court, centre left, which in Elizabethan times had connections with Russian merchants; the first Russian ambassador to the English Court also lived there. The Port of London Authority has control of the River Thames from Teddington to the sea, and the magnificence of its new headquarters reflected its influence on one of the world's greatest ports. The stone-fronted building overlooking the building site is Trinity House which is responsible for coastal lighthouses, lightships and buoys. The trees mark the presence of Trinity Square, the site of the scaffold where those executed outside the Tower of London on Tower Hill breathed their last. Trinity Square Gardens contains memorials to 36,000 members of the Merchant Navy and fishing fleets who lost their lives during two world wars.

Tower Hill, c. 1921. The Port of London Authority building was nearing completion, but the old warehouses on the left would linger on until after the Second World War. A modern entertainment for visitors, the Tower Experience, is here now together with a subterranean shopping mall and refreshment stalls. The was the boundary between the City and the old borough of Stepney, now Tower Hamlets. The Tower of London, off the picture to the right, is just outside the City of London.

Tower Hill, c. 1920. The Tower of London lies behind the trees on the left, which border its moat. To the right, the houses and shops were all that remained of a long-vanished road called George Street. There are now gardens, a new Tower Hill Underground station and an impressive section of Roman wall which had previously been hidden by George Street's houses. With its unmatched historical treasures, this part of London is one of the most popular with visitors, one of whom is seen on the far left consulting a rather unruly map.

Aldgate Pump, c. 1920. Leadenhall Street, left, and Fenchurch Street, right, merge to become Aldgate by Aldgate Pump, a landmark in the eastern part of the City. The Aldgate Well was mentioned as early as the thirteenth century. The buildings here have mostly gone or been rebuilt and a widened Aldgate now reveals a fine view of the eighteenth-century St Botolph's church.

Bishopsgate Street Within, (now Bishopsgate), c. 1896. Bishopsgate was once home to several wealthy City merchants, and part of one of the grandest of their mansions, the gabled Crosby Hall, is seen centre right. It was built for Sir John Crosby between 1466 and 1475 and was partly destroyed in the seventeenth century, but the spectacular stone-built hall survived here until 1908 when its site was needed for a new bank. Fortunately, the hall was dismantled and re-erected in Cheyne Walk, Chelsea, where it still stands.

Guildhall, c. 1920. The centre of the City's civic government, Guildhall dates from around 1411, but its frontage to Guildhall Yard was given the more modern look we see here in 1788. This was partly removed in Victorian times but restored in 1910. Demolition of the Guildhall Justice Room in the 1970s has opened out a grand view of Guildhall's medieval walls from an enlarged Guildhall Yard. A new building scheme is currently providing a new art gallery for the Guildhall collection, which was housed in the old gallery to the right.

Queen Street from Cheapside, c. 1920. Queen Street, with King Street, was created after the Great Fire as a new route from the Thames to Guildhall. This view shows a typical City shop and office mixture, with the picture-filled windows of Gladwell & Co., the print sellers on the Cheapside corner, attracting lively interest. The all-male City crowd is sporting a variety of headgear.

Fore Street, *c.* 1925. The great days of Fore Street ended long ago. Here was the birthplace of Daniel Defoe, and until the nineteenth century it was the busiest shopping street in the northern part of the City. By 1925, most of the buildings were workshops or offices, but worse was to come when the Blitz left it all in ruins. New buildings filled a much truncated Fore Street with uninspiring office blocks, but there was some welcome greenery by the Barbican's residential Andrewes House. The sloping boards on the left had mirrors on their upper sides to reflect daylight into gloomy rooms.

London Wall from Moorgate Street, *c.* 1925. London Wall follows the line of the City's northern fortifications which may still be seen at several points along its length. This is the street's eastern part which still has buildings of a similar scale. A post-war road scheme extended London Wall westwards as a dual carriageway to Aldersgate Street running beside and beneath a majestic cityscape of towering office blocks at the southern boundary of the Barbican.

Tranter's Hotel in Bridgewater Square, Barbican, *c*. 1908. The temperance hotel run by George Tranter occupied one side of this once residential square which had been built on the site of Bridgewater House, the town house (burnt down in 1687) of the Earls of Bridgewater. Although the houses have long gone, Bridgewater Square's name survived the transformation of acres of surrounding bomb sites into the futuristic residential and arts complex of the Barbican when many other local street names were lost.

Aldersgate Street, Barbican, *c*. 1920. Not a brick remains of this scene following its wartime destruction and subsequent rebuilding. On the right was Aldersgate Underground station which was bombed, rebuilt and in 1968 renamed Barbican. The Victorian Gothic Manchester Hotel no longer graces the Long Lane corner and the buildings on the left have been replaced by the Barbican's western boundary leading to the Museum of London. Barbican was once the name of a street (seen left); this is now part of Beech Street, which runs beneath the elevated world of the new Barbican.

Excavating the Temple of Mithras, Walbrook, 1954. Many centuries of accumulated debris has given the City a ground level many feet above that of Roman times. A cleared building site gives archaeologists the chance to explore the City's buried past and in 1954, such a dig revealed the remains of a third-century Mithraic temple which the Romans built on the banks of the Walbrook stream. Mithras was the ancient Persian god of heavenly light, and was one of the deities worshipped by the Roman legions. The reconstructed remains of the temple can be seen in Queen Victoria Street.

Excavating the Roman wall, Newgate, *c.* 1903. The size and thickness of the wall is shown well here and gives us an idea of the immensity of the task the Romans embarked upon when they encircled their city in this way.

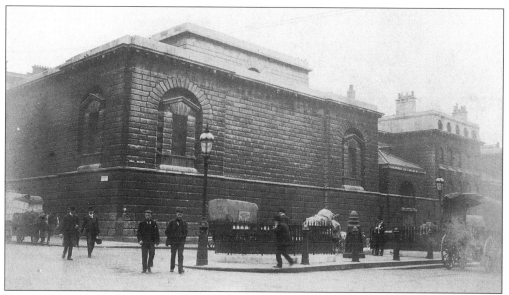

Newgate Prison, Newgate Street, by Old Bailey, *c.* 1901. Suitably grim and forbidding, the fortress-like walls of Newgate reflected the long history of this place as a prison from the twelfth century. The building we see here dated from 1780, and in front of it was London's principal place of execution following the abandonment of Tyburn. Newgate Prison was demolished in 1902, the site then being used for the Central Criminal Court, the Old Bailey, which was opened in 1907 by King Edward VII.

The Central Criminal Courts, the Old Bailey, from Holborn Viaduct, *c.* 1920. The nation's more notorious criminals have been tried here including Crippen, Christie, the Yorkshire Ripper and wartime Nazi propagandist Lord Haw-Haw. A plaque in the building's wall records the site of Newgate, an entrance (demolished in 1777) in the City wall. The church of St Sepulchre-without-Newgate, left, the site of a church since Saxon times, dates in part from the fifteenth century.

King Edward Street from Little Britain, c. 1904. With the unsavoury slaughterhouses of the Newgate Shambles close by, the street was known at various times as Stinking Lane, Chick Lane and Blowbladder Street. It was later called Butchers Hall Lane due to the proximity of that Livery Company's hall. The street was finally named after Edward VI, who in 1552 founded Christ's Hospital nearby. In this photograph, demolition of old property on the right was clearing the way for the King Edward Building of the GPO, whose foundation stone was laid by Edward VII on 16 October 1905. The National Postal Museum with its unique collections of stamps and postal history is housed there now. Angel Street, in the centre, was named after a local inn. Everything else has been rebuilt other than St Paul's, which still commands the skyline.

St Bartholomew's Hospital, 1939. London's beloved 'Barts' was founded in 1123, the same year as the church of St Bartholomew-the-Great, on the left. The tower of the hospital's own parish church, St Bartholomew-the-Less, dating in part from the fifteenth century, is on the right. The building appeal banner over the hospital's main entrance reminds us that the hospital gate 'has not closed in 816 years'. This, however, was 1939 and with war just months away, the skill of Barts' doctors and nurses was about to be called upon as seldom before.

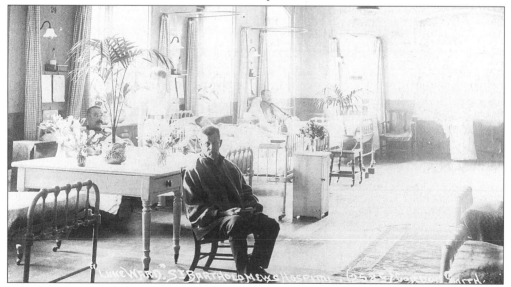

Luke Ward, St Bartholomew's Hospital, c. 1906. Wooden tables, iron beds, rugs on the floor and plenty of pot plants – this is a typical Edwardian hospital ward.

Cloth Fair, West Smithfield, *c.* 1910. With tall, partly wooden houses facing each other across a narrow roadway, Cloth Fair was one of the last streets of seventeenth-century houses in the City to survive into the twentieth century. The row on the left which backed onto St Bartholomew's churchyard did not last much longer, but the houses on the right survived for eventual restoration in what is now an exceedingly picturesque corner of the City. The north porch of St Bartholomew's was built in 1893 on the site of another old house which jutted out, considerably narrowing the road. The name Cloth Fair is derived from the largest cloth market in this country which was held here from the twelfth century, and was of sufficient stature to attract cloth merchants from many parts of the continent. The view is looking towards West Smithfield and shows Sun Court (now Rising Sun Court) on the right. Sir John Betjeman, the twentieth century Poet Laureate who loved these ancient corners of the City, lived in a house by Cloth Court, in the centre of the picture.

Cloth Fair, *c*. 1910. Looking in the opposite direction from the same spot reveals more of Cloth Fair's historic houses. Many of the old shops provided services associated with the meat trade in nearby Smithfield Market. Those on the right backed up against the walls of St Bartholomew's church which was revealed in all its splendour when the houses were eventually pulled down. The overhanging upper storeys of the fifteenth-century Ye Olde Dick Whittington pub ('the oldest licensed house in the City of London') can just be seen by Kinghorn Street, centre. It has sadly gone as have the other buildings on the left, and there are smart new town houses here now. Facing the camera in the distance on the Middle Street-Kinghorn Street corner was a useful local amenity, William Phelan's grocery shop.

Holborn Viaduct from Farringdon Street, *c.* 1875. The spanning of the steep-sided valley of the River Fleet, or Hole Bourne as this reach of it was called, was one of the great Victorian street improvements in the City. Previously, the traffic had to negotiate the treacherously graded Holborn Hill and Snow Hill. The viaduct runs from Holborn Circus to Newgate, but most of it is hidden by the buildings erected against it – it is only at Shoe Lane and Farringdon Street that the sides of it can be seen. Holborn Viaduct was designed by William Heywood and opened by Queen Victoria on 6 November 1869, a busy day for Her Majesty with Blackfriars Bridge to open as well.

The first bus over Holborn Viaduct, 8 November 1869. The driver of the bus was Thomas Grayson, who as a memento of the occasion was presented with a gold-mounted whip by his passengers. Thomas Grayson was an enterprising chap who added to his income by selling these souvenir photographs of himself and his bus.

Holborn and Staple Inn, *c.* 1904. London's finest Elizabethan façades are part of Staple Inn and are familiar far beyond the City from their depiction over many years on Old Holborn tobacco packets. The buildings have been restored many times and were rebuilt in 1937, ensuring the continued survival of the façades behind which the new building was constructed. The photograph shows a typical City contrast of the old co-existing with the latest technology, which in Edwardian times meant one of London's first street telephone kiosks, right.

Staple Inn Hall, *c.* 1910. Staple Inn was an Inn of Chancery from 1378 to 1884. Its buildings are now home to the Institute of Actuaries. The sixteenth-century hall was destroyed by a flying bomb on 24 August 1944 but was rebuilt with such skill in 1955 using salvaged materials from the old hall that this idyllic scene appears little changed. In his novel *Edwin Drood*, Charles Dickens comments on the tranquillity of this place just yards from the clamouring traffic of Holborn.

Mansion House, *c.* 1926. Mansion House, left, is the official residence of the Lord Mayor of London and was built between 1739 and 1753 on the site of the Stocks Market which stood here from 1282 to 1737. Mansion House also used the site of St Mary Woolchurch Haw, an ancient church destroyed in the Great Fire and not rebuilt. Mansion House was designed by the Clerk of the City Works, George Dance, with a relief by Robert Taylor above the portico representing the dignity and opulence of the City. The building with the circular tower, centre, was occupied by Mappin & Webb, the jewellers, but the City is the poorer for the recent demolition of this remarkable Victorian corner. Poultry (named after the old poulterers' market), Cheapside and St Mary-le-Bow are also seen, and to the right, with only one building, is the shortest main road in the City, Mansion House Street.

Acknowledgements

I would like to offer my sincere thanks to Judges Postcards Ltd, Hastings (01424-420919), Tony Davies of Marylebone Gallery and R.W. Kidner for their pictorial contributions to this book, and to transport historians R.W. Kidner and David Brewster for their invaluable help and advice. Special thanks are also due to Guildhall Library, the Museum of London and Westminster Archives Centre. Books consulted include the indispensable *The London Encyclopaedia* by Ben Weinreib and Christopher Hibbert; *The Buildings of England – London*, *vol. 1* by Nikolaus Pevsner and Bridget Cherry; *London Underground Stations* by David Leboff; *The Square Mile* by Warren Grynberg; *Discovering London Street Names* by John Wittich; *Walks in Old London* by Peter Jackson; *City of London Churches* by John Betjeman.